Aeolian Harp
volume 2

Edited by Lois P. Jones & Ami Kaye

Guest Editor: Lois P. Jones
Series Editor: Ami Kaye
Project Manager: Royce Ellen Hamel
Layout, Book & Cover Design: Steven M. Asmussen
Copyediting: Linda Kim
Cover Artist: Tracy McQueen

Fonts "National Oldstyle", "Persnickety", and "Metro Thin" designed by Andrew Leman, courtesy of The H. P. Lovecraft Historical Society, www.cthulhulives.org

Aeolian Harp Series: Anthology of Poetry Folios
Volume 2
Copyright © 2016 Glass Lyre Press, LLC
Paperback ISBN: 978-1-941783-28-3

All rights reserved: except for the purpose of quoting brief passages for review, no part of this book may be reproduced or transmitted in any form or by any means, electronic or mechanical, including photocopying, recording, or by any information storage and retrieval system, without permission in writing from the publisher.

Glass Lyre Press, LLC
P.O. Box 2693
Glenview, IL 60026

www.GlassLyrePress.com

Preface
Ami Kaye, Series Editor

The Aeolian Harp series was conceived with the idea to present a closer look at a poet's work in a more intimate setting. This second volume comprises the folios of ten poets: folios brimming with worlds of ideas and images, as engaging as they are diverse. Some are hushed meditations, some filled with humor and joy, and some are strong and strident voices to awaken our senses. All of these poets are visionaries in their own way, participating fully in the business of life.

In order to select ten folios for this unique format, we were forced to turn away a quantity of excellent work. As always, we thank the authors who sent us their folios for consideration; in submitting their fine work, they have raised the bar.

This type of project requires an editor with deeply refined yet diverse sensibilities and Lois P. Jones, with her numerous gifts, goes the extra mile. Her tireless diligence, thoughtful analysis, and natural sense of poetics made it possible to deliver a publication of high caliber. We are endlessly grateful for her editorial acumen and generous spirit.

In recent times, with daily explosions of violence and conflict, poetry provides a place for people to face their innermost feelings and thoughts. Since poetry taps into our primal emotions, it has the power to connect us. Through poetry and the arts we can share messages of hope, strength, and solidarity. When the world seems to fall around us and we feel troubled and uneasy, doubting our future and very existence, Marie-Elizabeth Mali's wisdom reminds us not to lose hope or turn our backs. It reminds us that good can come from bad, that beauty lives in strange places, and that when a wound is inflicted its salve might also be found:

> "Praise this beautiful, terrible world where we are opened
> and crushed, where the kiss comes from a mouth that bites."

Foreword
Lois P. Jones, Guest Editor

"The Poets light but Lamps —
Themselves — go out —
The Wicks they stimulate
If vital Light

Inhere as do the Suns —
Each Age a Lens
Disseminating their
Circumference

    — Emily Dickenson

    The analysis of this one short poem by Dickenson could (and has) offered pages of distillation to consider. Within its profound proposals is the question of what makes poetry visible. What light is necessary to see? One aspect is the dynamic interplay between words as symbols and our interpretation of their sense and meaning. It's as if words were wicks and our minds the match. Let's say the other elements of poetry—sound, meter, syntax, color, tone, form, etc.—are part of the wick raiser which turns the flame of the lamp up or down. How much light is allowed into the mind's room and how much is left to our imagination?

    In the second quatrain, Dickenson broadens the concept of light to encompass the lens. The lens of the poet is not only limited or expanded by the poet's own perception, but by what he or she allows you to see. In a recent *New York Times* article, "Why Poets Can Make Better Search Engines," poet and CEO of Kensho, Daniel Nadler, notes that our lives are awash in the familiar. He feels that poetry in particular was so good at defamiliarization that it was "the role that art in general and poetry specifically must play in the 21st century…as a counterweight to the many things pushing to decrease the length of perception." Adding to this are the ways in which poetry causes us to expand beyond our basic senses. A philosopher once named many of these perceptions: rhythm, smell, personal emotion, compass direction, and level of consciousness. I add to this a sense of time. How is it that day after day I wake up at different moments and my awareness of time is correct often within two to three minutes? These are random times! 7:45. 8:47. 9:34. What allows us to perceive beyond the physical world? How can I know when a family member across the distance is sad or troubled? Let's talk about the light in much broader strokes. Let's look at the circumference of our knowing and our ability to permeate one another's worlds, including individual creations. Why, when we read a line like Ocean Vuong's "The cathedral in his sea-black eyes," do we feel as if a perfectly round stone has dropped into a well so deep we may never know its end?

This is the mystery of poetry. Coleridge said, "Poetry is at its best when it's not completely understood." To which author and poet Jennifer Clement added, "But it has to be mystery that you trust, mystery that is close to faith. A good poem is a mystery you trust." This is where we enter the world of our five foloists. Each poet plays with the instrument of light, allowing the lens to open and close so that we may know more of ourselves and one another, and yet retain a sense of mystery (shadow) in which the reader may travel. Words shed a certain amount of light. Sometimes it is just a candle, and other times there is a conflagration of brilliance which lights the way.

Opening the volume with poet Sandra Marcetti is the perfect lamp to guide us:

> Like a plume
> of lemon in water
> or Champagne
> in a new flute,
> lumen sinks to
> ascend. A bee
> slips the glass,
> blinking within,
> brights bubbling
> from the hand.

Look and listen to the beauty of these lines—the assonance and elegance of flute, plume, and lumen. The way the side glance of hand makes one think of land. If lumen is the measure of light emitted by its source, then this poet places us directly within its effervescence. We are drunk in its bright bubbling. Swept up in its glistening plume. Marcetti's work stirs the poetic palette in ways that seem to defy definition. It feels at moments like absolute music—elemental—a kind of metrical tuning fork that rings within our silence. I feel an excitement within the lines along with the poet's masterful control as each slender line coaxes the reader to the next.

Wherever Marcetti turns, there is luminosity. As when the fox in "Shadow" engages her and the lens opens cinematically into "the silver-eyed murderer/who smells breath in the air." And later in "Amberwing," ever conscious of the subtle play of gleam and gloss in its opening directive—"Hover over me, / fat-beaded miracle"—she balances the supernal within a darker counterpoint:

> I limb the path, black;
> across the rim,
> the petals of a rose
> close at the edge

And somewhere Ezra Pound and Elisabeth Bishop are nodding their heads and agreeing, "Yes, this is the stuff."

It is a natural leap to transition into Lia Brooks' portentous turns. Like Ted Hughes, her poems are lush with symbolism and bursting with the dark imagery of nature and the English landscape. There is a dynamic pacing and language. A precision which allows the tightrope to be navigated, knowing any loss of control might find her reader in the abyss between abstraction and meaning. In "Sink Eels," Brooks captures a moment of slow implosion. As the moment opens, there is something between dread and astonishment as sunlight tricks the mind into shadowy lines that make their way into the poet's consciousness, becoming eels which "lose their light tocsin / in this wet sediment, oozing down the sides, tugging / their open mouths behind them." It is a prime example of the way in which poetry can express the transmogrification of our senses, merging the past with the present as our sense of linear time is upended.

Brooks' poems have a certain hypnotic tenor where mood is carefully tended in the land. She plays with light expertly not only in the literal sense of illumination and shadow, but in what is revealed. There is an uneasiness, but it is never flagrant or violent. It is in the tension of the line and image. We turn corners of surprise and foreboding, as in the worrying poem entitled "The Flood" where "somewhere on the wind / we hear a man crying. It's the useless part of a voice / that grants nothing but a stoop...." And further, "At night, the haunting/ blows hard in my head like the wind / through the lone oak—long spent, hollow / through its younger rings and struck by lightning."

In "Elk," a dark imaging of nature continues with a "sky shifting across / the mirrors of the pupils as if the world / passes then, one last time, its wild expanse." Metaphorically the weight of the elk's head compares with the heaviness of its subject. Whether it is the wounding of a wild nature or the underpinning constriction of lethal liaisons, the poet moves skillfully, surprisingly from the real to the supernatural, shifting language as she shifts the weight of meaning.

If the 21st century is anything, it is a relentless high beam on our past, compelling us to coax truth from its shadowy cave and take ownership of it. Lynne Thompson does this without affectation. We are planted firmly within the 19th century Afro-Jamaican diaspora where individuals made their way to North America despite the litany of horrific crimes, prevailing lynch laws, and the widespread subjugation of people of color. Still, the subject's father, "born to got nothing in a British colony," came to America in search of a better life. Even as the truth of these offenses sting us, the poet's skillful use of an almost Haibun-like form allows for an interplay of narrative and condensed lyricism to volley the reader from emotion to emotion:

…I came for four years to earn money teaching grammar and numerals the way I taught grammar and numerals to youngsters back home, knowing few black boys in the States were allowed to attend school, not knowing if any school would hire me….

> *The twins, color and cry,*
> *steal each other's breath, yet they*
> *grow under heaven.*

Thompson's folio evinces a love of language steeped in authenticity. She plays with voice and persona, with rhythms that are all sass and dare as in "How I Learned Where We Come From:"

> When she wants him for the late meal, she calls
> *supper soon Kingstown-man, curried goat, sticky-wicket*
>
> and he responds, testy, *not yet ready, Bequia-woman,*
> *Anglican church, basket with no handles.*

Thompson says in "Wishbone," "All I have is a drawer / of fetching charms." What she does not say is that by opening the drawer a reader falls into its constellation of keepsakes, which wisen and move us as much as they seduce our deeper natures.

For an artist known for his poignant fields of color as well as an unconventional catalogue of work, poet Sharon Venizio enters Rothko's work bravely with only a flashlight and a satchel of words to bring forth a sense of shape, emotion, and meaning to the artist himself. Her work is reminiscent of Rothko's process where an ekphrastic composition, an abstract figure, can be hinted at with color and light:

> ...no body no frame just rooms of color pulsating against each other like earth and sky a window of blue opens upward blurs into orange: this is breathing look how yellow is eaten by red nothing left but a burning house a mouth speaking: this is remembering
>
> his name no longer a word

I want to quote the entire poem, but what is the point? You want to step into Venizio's chapel and let these smart bombs (words) find their fusion. Be their own prayer. Her work feels deeply kinesthetic, centered by the physical world. Other poems of reckoning and loss are deftly drawn, whether she speaks of a parent's death at an early age, or of ghosts with a haunting, elusive splendor:

> Your ghost is an unkindness
> of ravens contained like a photograph
> moody with shadow. Your ghost
> is an ancient tree
>
> with nests of hair that flame
> white hibiscus, the flowers still bloom
> the garden with light.

Cities are opened. Galleries are opened. Waterways, trails, and bridges are opened. Windows, flowers, and lenses are opened. In a title which seems paradoxical, Alan Johnston decrees that "War is Opened," yet this opening reads like an unleashing, a pox, a Pandora's box strewn with post-modern debris. Messages reach us subliminally through dense urban imagery—each one detonating our angst and sense of helplessness (even a macabre sense of humor), as if we are tossed into a Dystopian age where our senses are under constant assault:

> In these messages bearing the mess
> of post-deconstruction, any Burning Bush
> is God.

There is tremendous richness in this sense of frenzy, even in the poet's own zone of creation where modern aesthetics dictate a subjugation of the I:

> War is opened on grammaticity,
> sign of the times, the cleanly concocted
> and clearly depersonalized zone of the poet

Yet Johnston retains both a sense of absurdity and wonder in these poems. Notice Johnston's marvelously droll "Attacking Solipsism with Flour Tortillas:"

> My English acquaintance called it "flaw."
> I say "flour," naming the name
> of all that blooms, scouring the vowel,
> a rounded mouth murdering English
> English, pistil tongue ululating beneath
> teeth

Even his titles draw mirth, evoking his passion for the palette. "Eater of the Avocadoes" is a slightly self-mocking, reverent ode to our favorite green fruit, and contains all the ingredients for devotion, flirting with a taste for Zen and redemption:

> philosopher of flavor,
> Dogen, eminent Buddha,
> jade or emerald, purchase of price --
> rough alligator texture
> of the throwaway skin.

The last poem of this set returns to war, but it is truly as its title suggests: "A Meditation on Bliss." Johnston suggests that "War was invented by the flowers / as the English and Aztec knew." He tells us that bliss "…knows / the bloom of dust borne up by the bullet / that misses its mark, / and leaps in joy / as the target stumbles beyond the sights."

Amen to that.

Is it not thus: deep inside, everyone is like a church, and the walls are decorated with splendid frescoes. In first childhood, when all the festiveness still lies open, it is too dark inside to see the paintings. ...Fortunate, however, the person who feels, finds and secretly uncovers it. He bestows gifts upon himself. And he will return home into himself.

—Rainer Maria Rilke

If there is a poet who has returned home, it is Lisken Van Pelt Dus. I would suspect given the luminosity and sacred tone of her writing, she never left it at all. Van Pelt Dus' hands hold both the lamp and the frescoes in full view so each reader may take part in its narrative scenes and artistry. In "It began Without Either of Us Knowing," the paradox of our spiritual connections within the physical world lulls us into that fifth dimension where presence is the curtain blown gently within and without the window of time:

> The knowing hid in the lace of our shadows
> Swallows flew in and out of our mouths
> Built nests in our throats
>
> We followed the birds into chimneys
> Flower-pots held our histories
> The sky threaded with geranium scent held our histories
> We weren't sure what was past and what was future
> So we were often silent

Van Pelt Dus' poems are elemental, yet complex, opening and revealing our vulnerable selves "(a)s if flesh were permeable— / not flesh exactly, but the whole body / we carry around, / what we feel with...." There is no dunnage to pad metaphor or meaning. Because of the poems' spare and specific language, I dare not quote extensively—better to read them within the context of their luminous whole. Their clean lines offer maximal power to permeate and inform the clarity and texture of their space. It is here where "Light opens, vertical / like your body," and within the poet's limning, we are transparent, transformed.

Lisa Cihlar's elegant prose poems are stylish portmanteaus. Not in an effete sense, but in the way that each piece contains what is necessary for the reader's journey without providing every detail. This type of poem has a difficult task: it must evoke a sense of story and lyricism within a small frame. And so they do. They are also rich with rhythm and careful composition. Listen to the music in "Eskars and Drumlins:"

> This land hump is a knife-edge slicing between growing lavender and killing lavender.

You could almost dance to it. In the length of a line, the poet's lens widens just enough to display a trousseau of memory, yet hints at tension and a small madness as we consider the edge of growing and killing lavender. And later:

> More often she sends him to the dovecote to leave seeds and fresh water. Everything about him hurts her memory.

Is "him" a son, a sibling, a partner? This is the satisfaction of a good prose poem. We are left to piece together the story left by subtle hints of characters and location, enabling a landscape—a texture—not only of place but of thought, allowing for enough mystery to satisfy us. The poems seem to operate in a sustained reality that ventures into a kind of magical ontology.

In "The Last Catydid," the poet speaks of the "bear in my life" and how she "keep[s] a fire burning to stave off hibernation." Look at the light in these few lines:

> Hollyhocks have stopped self-seeding, all of the crickets have died, and the hens' combs are frostbitten. They are still laying five pure white eggs and one blue egg each day. The chicks were darling fluffs at the co-op. I can't remember their fancy names. Just that I wanted lemon curd and bright golden yolks. Eggs are both sun and moon.

"Eggs are both sun and moon." These are the kinds of surprises we leap to in good poetry, and our lens widens and we say, "More please, just like this."

We all remember the line from the film *Jerry Maguire*: "You had me at 'hello.'" Alison Stone's opening to "Yes" shows us the money with its immediacy and cockeyed view:

> Love is a room I enter sideways.
> Roots of gut, branches of bone,
> our bodies burn like trees.

What do we wish from a poem? Personally, I want the poet, in most cases, to bypass exposition. I want to be inside the poem from beginning to end. I want to be slayed, line by line. Stone's poem accomplishes all of this. The entire poem is quotable—haunting in its metaphysical reach.

More of these folio pieces turn on a coin of desire and satisfaction. In the tender "Hunger," loss and gain live side by side: "They have to wait to bury my mother / until my daughter stops nursing." The balance played here hovers as the poem itself does between this world and the next. Sometimes there is an irony in the act of aging—a teasing wit not without its murkier side:

> Vulnerable to you, I might become
> one of those moon-faced women, wounded
> and obvious, spilling out of a loose dress.

The last poem, "Perimenopause," anchors as it buoys, "as a womb frantic/with final eggs" urges and insists, yet retains a primal incandescence.

Beth Copeland's folio is elegy and homage with a twist of good humor to keep perspective on her subjects. These poems speak to loss of life of the still living—the ebb of memory and the irony of erasure. If you have the opportunity, please take a few moments to view the Motionpoems video created for her "Falling Lessons: Erasure One" (not included in this folio), featured on the PBS News Hour. In this article, Copeland reveals that before her father's death

> ...she wrote a longer narrative piece about the last few years of his life. But then, she did something unusual: she deleted most of it. That process of erasure was a way to put herself in her father's place, replicating what had happened as his disease progressed.

This is surely an act of bravery and of faith in Copeland's ability to harvest remnants of her memory and trust that the process will pan its own gold.

She delivers.

The poems in this folio shift between aging parents and her history sewn metaphorically into their pattern. "Featherweight Singer" brings the tactile and sounds of the old world into the present when parents and grandparents sewed clothing by hand, and a child might be lulled into its safety:

> I fell
> asleep to the white noise of that
>
> black machine, to the song of steady
> seams like wind in cottonwoods
>
> or rain on rafters, to my mother's breathing
> when I climbed her bed after bad dreams.

In "Keeping Time," memory is not the only thing which is illusive. Moments bend in the details: "(t)he clock / doesn't advise / me to stay or leave, his watch / somewhere still keeping time." The lines speak so well to our desire to connect despite knowing otherwise. A new reality is created within the poet's lines where time is a kind of fractal in a pattern of forgetting.

The last poem, my favorite of the group, reminds us that light and color are what make a Vermeer immortal. If Girl With a Pearl Earring in its patterns of delft blue and gold, its museum light cast tenderly on the face tell us that the painting is more a portrait of a relationship than of a person, then "Sandhills Gold" is a portrait of a connection between father and daughter and its immutable splendor:

> I spoke
>
> of his veiled hat and long gloves,
> bellowing hives
>
> with smoke so he could pull combs and

honey from inside, and pour sourwood

into old Mason jars in slow motion
like the lengthening summer day

when the sky was so delphinium
it could be music

Peter Ludwin's light burns resplendent; it is often ecstatic, yet grounded in history and place. By the way his work unfolds, you can tell he is an experienced storyteller: a raconteur that says as much about the man as the work itself. Ludwin is a poet who appreciates both the narrative arc and the unexpected leap into duende. In "Arrow Flight," one imagines the young boy alive with the music of language, bunkered down in the belly of an Old Nordic tale where "[t]hose old / Germanic tribes knew how to do it right. / When Beowulf died they carried his body down / to the beach, placed it on a boat with his armor, / torched it and set it adrift." And later in the same poem, Ludwin reflects on the parallel universe of the father and the darker fates:

> You couldn't see their eyes drain the blood
> from dark rivers, couldn't hear the jackal's bark
> when they tossed the ashes like an old, broken-spring
> clock that lacked even the memory of leaves.

Here is that fine leap into oblivion where an old broken spring clock lacks the memory of leaves. That is the lightening right there. It is a kind of understated spontaneous combustion where the reader suddenly questions what they read, reads it again, and thinks about the frictional elements of words—how if you choose just the right handstone and just the right striker, the spark will leap to the mind's fire.

Ludwin's other tools are the elemental blends of color and sound. As in "Blue Mosque" where east truly meets west. Where the musician takes over and words become a riff of spontaneous associations (let's call them leaps in the tradition of Bly), moving us through a mosaic of sensory extremes:

Say *blue*, and doors swing wide open.

To speak it here adds yet another
tile to the thousands already present.
Did Gershwin divine such a rhapsody?
Such a dazzling faience mosaic?
Or is blue encoded in our cells,

a script for the primal color of being?

And now we approach perhaps the most dynamic aspects of Ludwin's craft – transcendence. How the earthly gives over its gifts through "a long corridor of trees… wearing a mantle of low clouds." Where collapsed barns wear the ghosts of desire and rosehips "…singe your fingers like frost."

> We are reminded of why were are here—
> to get things down, to leave a mark, an imprint,
>   …in a voice that insists, …ah, Consuelo, mi vida,
> I was here, I sang your song.

Aeolian Harp is a unique creation drawn together without attention to ego or cachet but a desire to gather voices which resonate and cohere through the patient and caring direction of its creator. Rather than guide the ship, Ami lights the way for the best possible path toward unity and balance. There seems a magic to it. It's been an honor to witness Ami's discerning eye and highly-tuned aesthetics as we worked to create a cohesive collection within a marvelous format where each poet has their own dais and a spotlight to reveal their talents.

...this harp which I wake now for thee
  Was a siren of old who sung under the sea.

— Thomas Moore, *The Origin of the Harp*

Folios

Sandra Marchetti	13
Lia Brooks	21
Lynne Thompson	31
Sharon Venezio	41
Allan Johnston	49
Lisken Van Pelt Dus	59
Lisa J. Cihlar	67
Alison Stone	75
Beth Copeland	83
Peter Ludwin	95

Sandra Marchetti

Poetry is "it." We are not waiting for it, or reading ahead to get to it. Poems are the thing themselves, especially short poems. I am drawn to poetry because 50 words can do more than I ever dreamed when I think of them as a poem. Poetry makes an art of arrangement, of collecting. I get to keep the unusual and the beautiful in the wonder cabinet that is a poem.

Octavio Paz says, "Poetry is memory become image, and image become voice." That voice is the arrangement, the act of collecting. Paz mentions a Chinese saying that the poem unites the "ten thousand things that make up the universe." I agree that poems do more with less. They energize and fire our minds in ways that we can't imagine possible when we aren't reading poems. A poem is also a song that must make meaning and music using just one instrument—words.

After I shape a working draft, I usually "walk the poem." I take it for a walk, and time my steps to it. As a metrical poet, this really helps me. I can still confuse myself when I scan a poem with pen and paper silently, so reading a poem aloud is another method I use. I am not a musician, but I often feel like one. I also memorize my pieces. All of these physical and verbal acts help me to learn when stresses are off, and when they are clean. I oftentimes don't understand all of the sonic rhythms and how they work until the poem is nearly finished, since so much of this knowledge is bodily.

One of my poems is finished when it stops itching at me. When I stop thinking about that alternate ending, or am no longer scheming about a sharper verb or better turn of phrase, it's done. When I can read the piece aloud without stumbling, it's done. When I can tap my toe to it without worrying over the beat, it's finished. Better yet, when I stop doing all of these things and pick up the poem again to read it, and like it, I know it's there.

Gibbous

A column of light
smeared in Degas
style. Japanese paper
hanger's moon
through clouds.
Like a plume
of lemon in water
or Champagne
in a new flute,
lumen sinks to
ascend. A bee
slips the glass,
blinking within,
brights bubbling
from the hand.

Shadow

"Across clearings, an eye,"
—Ted Hughes, "The Thought-Fox"

Mushrooms on the trail indicate
you haven't roved this prairie of late;

soft-sponged and pink, they're sweet
as the berries ripped in your teeth.

"Foxes are opportunistic feeders,"
notes a sign—I never mind

the goldfinches who arc my breeze
and swap big bluestem for trees

patiently trilling each leaf, those
last full masts of September.

Zig-zagged grass ripples from a felled
trunk, sunk in its thatch to rot.

Past piles of branches spoiled
to mash, a flaxen hay

wherein I catch your gleam—
spun gold you are a long-bodied

beam, slinking past imagined
houses down to the stream.

Hidden to your scruff in the gathering
dusk, I hold and release your stare,

that of a silver-eyed murderer
who smells breath in the air.

Ebb Tide

Spiders wind behind limestone
at heights twice mine.

A black beach brines
the vine-choked wall,

times my dizzied pull
at the horizon line.

~

I tell you this time I am not afraid.
I click the teeth of seven gods,

catch vines in my throat
and spit them to the sea.

I tell you I spark into fire
the grass behind my strides.

AMBERWING
Perithemis tenera

Hover over me,
fat-beaded miracle.

Swell your breast
clustered between

red-tinged wings
in autumn nearly

done opening.
Scan the grass

one last time,
dry as a stone,

as a woman alone,
climbing the stairs,

landing nowhere.

Kaleidoscope

We're warned all water drains to sewers.
In rivers, fathers who escape
the house wash hands after weeding.

The run-off teems the flow:
Dillard's fish flashes
then dissolves like so much.

On the bank, men's shadows
beam as black bears might
upend themselves,

rocks in the stream,
their furred mouths
gleaming with the catch.

Soon

 with a line from Sylvia Plath

So shot with stalks
I can't see the garden
claimed from rock.

I will not press flesh
to grass, ruffled
thick to green, sleep

a finch feathered
through each fist.
My foot slips—

I'm china, discarded
under moonbeam.
I limb the path, black;

across the rim,
the petals of a rose
close at the edge.

Lia Brooks

Music has played a big part in my writing life. I started writing when I was small, with nursery rhymes and music as my main influences. I played piano and clarinet from this time, and also enjoyed sketching and painting. The land fascinated me. I heard sounds in it that I needed to put into words. I started to observe rhythms both in landscapes and seascapes. I wondered how we as people might fit into it. If we harboured similar rhythms. Since the beginnings of adulthood I've been trying to explain this relationship in my writing.

I have learnt that with or without the poem the poet is still a poet. It is something that defines a type of person rather than simply something they actively do. And if it is something that we are then the poem is the conversation – as if the poet sits down at a table with the reader and the conversation begins. Of the conversation, I suppose I want language to go to a place that I have never visited and to see what I cannot. For it to feel more than I am capable of, and to understand and accomplish more than I ever could. The land, first. Our place within it, second. And finally, that table I sit down at ready for the conversation to start.

The Sink Eels

A white sun arrows itself clean
through the window to the back of my hand,

popping soapsuds like blisters, leaking eels
over the sink edge. They lose their light tocsin

in this wet sediment, oozing down the sides, tugging
their open mouths behind them. I have been elver

colouring from glass and weaving just as loosely.
It was his shape, those years ago in the dark,

that made me less moray and all shock.
At the plug, I pour myself counter-clockwise

through the six holes, come out in the pipeway
divided, no part of me fluid enough to coalesce,

but as tails and bile heavy on the water's surface
as it makes its way underground. I'll be regurgitated –

some infectious froth squeezed back up
to stain the flat of the sink. On my back, eyes

and mud congealed, looking blindly at the artex,
unmovable in my white box, tap dripping on my feet.

Elk

Sometime later, the man appears from the trees
holding the head of an elk. The bare branch
of an antler scratches the ground, dragging
the debris of the woodland with it. See there
on both fat, black eyes the naked field,
the white band of sky shifting across
the mirrors of the pupils as if the world
passes then, one last time, its wild expanse.
In through the trees, in a quiet part
where birds look down
on the future of the body, hooves
jitter across pine-needles,
front leg bending at the knee until
the soft taupe stomach is on the ground.
Sometime earlier, the elk is in a similar place
foraging. It is thinking about the wind,
the drop in temperature, that it will rain
in an hour, maybe two. It is thinking
yesterday, in a similar place, there was food
enough for the mouth of its herd.
The elk listens then, its head pressed
to the wind, hears the hunger-calls of calves
winding through the darker parts of the wood.
When the new noise comes, the elk doesn't move –
already aware of the difference; the taste
in the air, the shift of the broom. The eyes
take the shape of the man without flinching. There is
no thought about running, only to wait
and look and wait; and this is how it is
every time you come home.

The Flood

The year the house floods, bees fall out of the sky.
Fat bodies land on the grass, each one
without a head. I step between them,

count nineteen and tell you
it's a mass suicide. Murder, you say afterwards.

The same year, I leave the lid off the water barrel.
A young blackbird floats on his back through mosquito
larvae, looks sideways at us from a drunken eye.

The mother, nesting in the bay-tree with twigs
and then worms, waits on the fence. The year water

rises over the step, seeps under the door and pulses
into our kitchen, the sky hollows out its length.
Neighbours puzzle over it as if May conjures

out of the budding stems and new sun
all of its emptiness and offers it up like a trick.

We are out walking and somewhere on the wind
we hear a man crying. It's the useless part of a voice
that grants nothing but a stoop. The echo sweeps

back into the trees and I have difficulty
losing it from my ears. At night, the haunting

blows hard in my head like the wind
through the lone oak – long spent, hollow
through its younger rings and struck by lightning. The nest

inside it, a throbbing heart, so hot
hornets leak from it, over the field and pour

into our garden, suck the heads off the bees
and spit them out like rain. The year the house floods
we are warned well enough a wave is coming.

You'd think about that long before me.
On the day of the flood, I wake late,

carry a mug of tea back to bed and look out
so the window is all sky. I am restless for the sea,
out of my mind for it, and never hear the fence give way.

Pendular Song of Summer

The mark on the counter-top is a heat stain—
palm then fingers

spread around it like a child's sun
and drying

in a summer afternoon until, soon,
there is only

the smoothness of marble, the silence
that follows

and a woman with her back to a doorway
made for children,

made to swing in and out of the room,
metronomic,

for each one that returned home. Sometimes,
she thinks,

the wind is a song sung by the soot-throat
of the chimney,

concertinas newspaper in the grate,
the kindling,

with logs enough to roar through the bricks,
smoke the notes

into the blistering July sky
above her house.

As land buries each task it has finished with,
the river

swerves and blinks beyond the garden fence,
the bullfrog flops

from the bank like a fat over-ripe pear,
alder leaves

heavy and green, the hot alder leaves
glittering.

The Land, For You

As if I put you to sleep
and placed seeds
over your eyelids
in a dark place
of the forest
somewhere far in
and surrounded by pines

As if I knocked an owl
from its branch
with a large stone
and when it was lifeless
pulled out every wing
and tail feather
and pressed them between your teeth

As if I piled brown leaves
at your feet
around your head
in a line across your chest
and let the woodlouse wander
as if across a great bridge
between Earth and its one whistling thought

As if I took a knife
to your third rib
dug out a sliver of bone
and replaced it
with an acorn
to store for the hours
in Winter's coldest dark

As if I snared a fox
undressed it from its skin
lay the pelt over you
and kept safe the arms
and legs of you
the mind and blood of you
from every skulking thing

As if I knelt down
and kissed your cold cheek
let you rest beneath the trees
until eight days later
found you sitting
among pine needles
with all the world at your mouth

Lynne Thompson

For me, the heartbeat of poetry lies within the stories it advances. Whether those stories are conveyed in a lyric narrative mode or via a more formal technique. Whether those stories engage with white space on the page or pull the reader through with traditional stanzaic formulations. And within the stories propelled by poetic line breaks is a certain—sometimes familiar, sometimes unfamiliar—rythmic strain that operates to keep the reader entertained, shocked, saddened, or delighted.

The poems in this folio are, in part, born from my interest in public history's intersection with personal experience. As Toni Morrison so memorably said "if there is a book that you want to read, but it hasn't been written yet, you must be the one to write it". These poems arise from that impulse. "Genesis", for example, follows my father's journey as an immigrant from the Caribbean to the U.S., recognizing the challenges he faced when he arrived. "How I Learned Where We Come From" meditates on my parents' unique voices as a way of understanding how their children formed their own styles. Finally, "To Blackness" is a defiant statement of pride in being a member of the African diaspora.

The other poems selected address another obsession: the eternal struggle to understand relationships between people and how, individually, we take them in at the same time that we attempt to answer the unanswerable. I do *try* to have a little fun with these issues, though, and that sense of humor is, hopefully, apparent, in a poem like "Before We Are Full of Rue" (who wouldn't want to arrive in the "swagger of night"?) and "Last Elegy For the Red Dress" (revisiting a theme begun in its earlier incarnation, "Elegy for the Red Dress"). Notwithstanding the fun, I always return to wondering why any of us do what we do, particularly when, as in "Wishbone", 'these storms present without solution'. In writing poems, I hope to find a solution or two.

Genesis

I

...on twenty-seven March, 1899, Dora rose from her pallet, came to squat, and my father flopped out like a fish. One month later, American Negroes fasted in protest of the lynch laws, but Daddy, born to got nothing in a British colony, took off nonetheless and despite everything...

> *all gurgle and shit,*
> *a wheel, turning, his eyes fixed,*
> *history nascent...*

II

"I left that floating hotel, the Van Dyck, to arrive—via Barbados—on the Isle of Tears, June, 1923, and I didn't care what. We'd heard the news back home about a black man, Sam Hose, lynched for killing his Georgia white employer. Hose was burned alive, his knuckles put for sale and that'll teach 'em at the local grocer's, but I came anyway..."

> *The journey of not*
> *knowing isn't bitter or*
> *a sweet seed, just chance...*

"...I came for four years to earn money teaching grammar and numerals the way I taught grammar and numerals to youngsters back home, knowing few black boys in the States were allowed to attend school, not knowing if any school would hire me..."

The twins, color and cry,
steal each other's breath, yet they
grow under heaven.

"I came despite the rebellions: the Robert Charles Riots, 1900, 28 dead; the Wilmington Insurrection, no official death count; Springfield, 1908; Houston, 1917; District of Columbia, 1919; and all the unnamed uprisings every year since and in between."

Time's a magician—
sleight of hand and a white mask—
black fingers, unbound.

III

"When I said *I will come back*, Dora shook her head and sobbed. I came anyway."

How I Learned Where We Come From

When she wants him for the late meal, she calls
supper soon Kingstown-man, curried goat, sticky-wicket

and he responds, testy, *not yet ready, Bequia-woman,*
Anglican church, basket with no handles.

We children, we laugh, head for the hills
and the tall sweet-grasses, listen for the lilt

of frangipani tantie. She call *come in now*
pigeon peas, mangoes, poor man's orchids—

then we run, for true, and supper is all
cassava root, callaloo, very little sugar cane

and we're in it all at once: choirsong above
Mt. Pleasant, Port Elizabeth, harp of Paget Farm

till Father, he say *no,* defends his slipped-on wishes
for Soufrière, Sans Souci, Wallilabou Bay

and so on into the evening, calypso and steel drums,
a little Rasta and Bob Marley for us young'uns

until, finally, we are no longer black ironwood—
wood that will not float.

BEFORE WE ARE FULL OF RUE

come to me in the swagger of night.
Whether you are struggling vampire
or foe or star-breath, come—oh yes—
when I am in the land of malfunction
and curious syntax, of Strayhorn played

on Saturn's rims, come, when late-light
is least opaque. When owls start their
hooting, come. Whether or not I agree,
come like you've come on no Saturday
night before and alone, or, if you must,

come with your hands full of thyme.
Stay until the metronome stops then start
that tango all over again. If you come
to me, I'll give you lusty pandemonium
because, after heat-hard hours, I become

most true. Before it is too late—(and
isn't it always much too late?)—come.
And when we are completely filled with
the rue of our felonies, of our fallibilities,
tide and turn, then come once more.

Wishbone

The problems I have are few
at this time:

>	an absurd arithmetic
>	of desire—
>	a certain political
>	absence.

These storms present
without solution:
all the lipstick in the world—
all the choirs and buttressing
of angels atop cathedrals—oh,
how easily women are fooled.

All I have is a drawer
of fetching charms.
Does anyone know
why I keep them:
satinwood, nails,
one camisole and its metal,
phylactery, this mousetrap?

Last Elegy for the Red Dress

Good morning Red Dress—
heavy with the sweat of
Love Wants to Dance. Scented
with the hopes of Shy Man, Bold Man,
Begged-To-Take-Me-Home Man.
Still crinkly-crumply down the back
from the hanker in their hands.

Good Morning Red Dress.
'Morning chase-me, take-me shoes.
Looks like you've been out on the town,
like you've been dipped and twirled,
Dizzy'd and Duke'd all night long,
like you can't hang between sweatsuits
and jeans—like you're another kinda gal.

Hello and hey there, Red Dress,
double strand of pearls, faded rose
perfume still clinging to the bodice,
the slip, the silk of the sleeve;
still molten to my hips, my breasts,
to the drum of my heart, hem
softly pleated to a permanent party.

Where've you been, Red Dress?
And why have you moved on without me?

To Blackness

As it happens, I have never tired of blackness—its Marcus Garvey,
Raisin in the Sun, Tuskeegee airmen. Its Strivers Row and liver lips;

its Dred Scott, Freedman's Bureau, Scott Joplin. Some say black is
swarthy, gloomy, evil, fiendish, but we all spring from the tribes—

Ashanti, Bobo, Fulani, Wolof—their cowrie shells and krobo beads
sewn into our fading fabric. I don't know much about my native blackness;

my daddy he say Igbo, the only word he can give me, but it's the only word
I need to get the old folks to remembering that in Igbo *ututu* is morning,

abali is night, and in any mirror, my *ihu*—my face—is always black.

Sharon Venezio

When writing, I try to let the poem lead and hope it ends up somewhere interesting. Even if I don't begin writing a poem with a specific meaning in mind, similar themes emerge: family relationships, loss, transience, grief, redemption, psychology, photography, and the natural world. I believe poems begin long before we sit down to write them. My first book of poetry, *The Silence of Doorways*, opens with a quote by John Berger: "The camera relieves us of the burden of memory." Poetry, too, attempts to preserve, like a photograph, but also destroy and recreate as both truth and fiction. I'm interested in how poetry interacts with personal history and memory, how its language can resist definition yet reveal ourselves to us with such precision and clarity. Language creates a world where anything is possible and one of the great pleasures of writing poems is the chance to be the architect of my own world. I love the multiplicity of language, how a poem can hold different meanings and become a space to contain the impossible, a place where we can talk to ghosts and shadow selves, a place to die and be reborn.

For Rothko

he begins with an outline of a person   a curved line   a circle   then an x over the whole thing   starts over   no body   no frame   just rooms of color pulsating against each other like earth and sky   a window of blue opens upward   blurs into orange: this is breathing look how yellow is eaten by red   nothing left but a burning house   a mouth speaking: this is remembering

his name no longer a word   *white cloud over purple*   breaks open into *blue yellow green on red*

unhinges   is an instrument to unword the mind   hovers in-between like an eye closing over a rectangular field of light

Snapshot in Sepia

I

Years ago, my mother closed her bedroom window
and never looked out again. She collapsed like a wave
folding inward. She said hope can be an anchor;
it's easier to just let go.

I was fourteen and just barely paying attention,
straddling Billy's bike seat
while he pedaled standing up.

As the world turned on the grainy screen
of my mother's TV, Billy and I watched leaves
circle down from the maple outside my bedroom window.
They'd land on the hood of the orange Cutlass,
gather like unopened letters.

II

Our house had a crawl space
we entered through a removable bookcase in the wall.
I'd scale suitcases and boxes of family photos
until I reached the end. I'd draw a window on the wall,

open it up, let the pretend breeze pour
over my face and body
like my mother in her secret life
breathing the salt air of the sea.

Now I stand at the edge of the ocean
scatter her memory like a constellation
splayed across the night sky,
like moonlight unstitching the stars.

Disquietude

For two months I've been living with monks.
No longer dizzy from the circle of worry,
I see truth in the order of things,
eat for the body, not the senses. Still

I crave the sky in my mouth, feel
Kerouac's fabulous roman candles explode
like spiders beneath my skin, wake

yawning for coffee, daydream
of curry and spice, make poems in my head
about the wild dishevelment of being,
that fierce blue drowning.

Of the ten defilements, passion is the one
I can't shake. In a month, I'll step out
of the forest, carry my longing home again.

The Flame

Night's wingspan, wide as moon,
stretches toward the horizon.
Your ghost is an unkindness

of ravens contained like a photograph
moody with shadow. Your ghost
is an ancient tree

with nests of hair that flame
white hibiscus, the flowers still bloom
the garden with light.

Each fall I eat the flowered flame
to forget you, petal by petal,
eat it down to its grief

o doomed lover
hold your face up to the sky
until it becomes the sky

Three Exits
after Nathalie Handal

Version One

Place a story in her ear,
be the salt on the back of her tongue.
Make too much noise.
Say goodbye, forget her name,
don't take a picture.

Version Two

Take a picture, write her name
on the back with a green gel pen,
slip it into your bag,
glance back
as you close the door.

Version Three

Say goodbye, but never leave.
Let night tell you who you are.
Unbutton her face, be the green thorn
piercing the small furious flap of her heart.

Returning #2

When my mother flew from the nest everything was an empty mouth,
my stomach nothing but wind and sky. My teenage body, like driftwood,
washed ashore into the arms of men. I wanted them wholly,
wanted them distant, wanted them floating on the shoreline
like a black box detailing the scenes of my disaster.

For years it was my job to pour alcohol into the empty
cups of men. I watched cobwebs gather in their hair.
Now I watch for a flame of wings in the backyard of my childhood
home, remember the place I dreamed away from,
the empty glass I held out to the world.

A woman in the kitchen is sewing grief into an empty mouth
with a certainty only the body knows. The way a Swallow
builds its nest of saliva and mud, a genetic map flapping in the brain.

This house is not a map. It is the shadow of a girl who woke up
with the world opening inside her like an unnamable star,
the endangered world spinning on its axis, listening for the flap flap flap of leaving.
This house is made of tripwire. Here, let me show you.

Allan Johnston

Much of my writing stems from momentary creation and/or reworking, but more recently I have moved toward direct and organized ordering of chaos. I like Kenneth Rexroth's description of poetry as vatic, and Gary Snyder's assertion that poetry should express archaic values realized in primary cultures. Poetry gives witness, sometimes of the interior or of momentary interactions of ideas and things flowing in moments of creation, and upholds vision states that subvert or indicate the artifice or metaphoric division that makes understanding available. Words articulate the ineffable, and also arguably have "dharma" as spoken or signed entities, as well as use in the destruction and reconstruction of significance, language, and representation. I try to capture nuances by digging to out the roots of meanings, sounds, emotions, images, etc. Sometimes spontaneity is all that is required.

If an idea takes you around a corner and confronts you with a large octopus, that's exciting, that's poetry. I've had moments writing when the words that came out to end the thought surprised me, and I was the supposed one doing the thinking. Maybe it is the "thoughts without a thinker" aspect of poetry that interests me.

War is Opened

It happens like this almost every time.
One thing, another; descent into reverie
after the panic. Train cars break up
in the slow-motion sun-colored ochre
under standards that defy the brightness
of logic. "War is opened," the headlines read.

Meanwhile, the ebullience of litter
spills from cardboard in every garbaged
bog of alley, and the electric
neon nervosity of it rings
the paths of felines that seek understanding
or at least discarded heads of fish.

In these messages bearing the mess
of post-deconstruction, any Burning Bush
is God. Then the mailman discounts
the whom on the brick-curbed, weather-stained letter
from all that can be granted to power
or at least the firmness of the cigarette.

War is opened on grammaticity,
sign of the times, the cleanly concocted
and clearly depersonalized zone of the poet,
as if all advertisement were schmaltz
instead of negation of the unwanted.
Was there a square bit of form shining forth?

Define it by number. Hence a logic
of meter, the scantron of art we can under-
take or at least -stand, since declaration
defines us and anyway here we are
with cats that at least know what they're after
among the backdoor discardings of flowers.

Ashes

In the circle the way
a group of stones might be
kissing each other just to
block the progress of
the spirit or just be
the stones here as they fell,
so to speak, or as earth
pushes them out of whatever

is under this land, I look
and know no stone will ever
stand for those whose ashes
have been cast on water,
I guess, since this is what
I was told the contract stated.
I wasn't there to verify.
I guess after the service

and cremation, the ashes
were taken on board the boat,
and out somewhere to the lea
of the Channel Islands and tossed.
That was as it should be.
Yet it seems so cold;
how could anyone act
in the way she did

walking along and dragging
me out in the wet night,
the house past the land for any
moment of any thought
that something could have been said
about how our lives had unfolded,

so that I doubt — anger being
the precise instrument it is —

that any revealing will now
make my heart any better
an instrument for knowing
how to survive or fiddle
as everything is going
up in the burning or coming
out of me, as if
from a handful of ashes thrown
across the scattering waters.

Attacking Solipsism with Flour Tortillas

I leave a trail of whiteness,
the flour leaking out of my hand
on the dark grain of the wooden counter —
a bestrewal of stars   Milky Way

                strange
    constellations

And with water and another hand,
foment a world — one gooey, pasty
ball *por las tortillas*
        de la masa harina

My English acquaintance called it "flaw."
I say "flour," naming the name
of all that blooms, scouring the vowel,
a rounded mouth murdering English
English, pistil tongue ululating beneath
teeth,
    thereby bringing
    name to the Humean
    flaw of perception
    created on table tops
    via these shifty
    sifted trails I now
    call con-
        stel-
            lations;

estes panes calientes, a knowledge
of hunger, a beasty feast, yeasty
or unleavened —

what of these grains,
        too fine to discern
        except en masse,
        vision or creation?
        What of perception?
        I defy solipsism:

a quick, hard rolling! A *pin*! A hot *pan*!

The Eater of Avocados

opening

The militant leaves try to disguise them
in small memos of jungle.
He is too clever; he brings ladders.
Reaching up, he finds them;
thumbs of another substance, coarse
and gangly, too awkward to twaddle.
Their freeing is easy, a twist, a technique.
With practice it comes to nothing.

As the knife easily passes
through the skin the fruit surrenders.
He opens the soft, lopsided round
to find the green sky,
a teardrop of taste
coddled in oily atmospheres
along the curved horizon:
                              sunrise!
The yellow illumes the hard and pithy
redolent football seed:

the tree is waiting
to get cracking.

eating

It brings forth the first word
in the alphabet of taste.
Soft with water and southern dust,
it calls for salt and lemon;

the red ghosts of powdered chilies
flavor the syllabation: *AH!*
shape of the tongue and mouth
that shy and round to the form of fruit,
a small, green, leather-cassocked monk
who advocates sensation: *VO!*
the oiled variations on
a theme that gleams on chins, greens teeth,
receives these flavors speaking of
the ease of eating: *CA!*
a crow's weight of fruit in trees
with spatula leafs; the spiced scent
of the orchards through which deer move:
DO! philosopher of flavor,
Dogen, eminent Buddha,
jade or emerald, purchase of price—
rough alligator texture
of the throwaway skin.

discarding

Round
of the green sky
thickens inside,
solidifies
with a soiled
atmosphere:

this fruit:
seed within

a planet swimming
in oil:

this then
is the secret
of the avocado:

Things to be done, things to be done, the world at large
resting as if under the too heavy necessity of change,
as if the weight of contradiction were bearing down like a large crack;
and then the smokiness enters the taste,
and then comes the slow loss
of softness in
these hard black fibers

Meditation on Bliss

"Why write about bliss? There's a war on!"

War was invented by the flowers,
as the English and Aztec knew.
Lavenders attacked jacarandas
with luscious scents and iodine.
Soon the rhododendrons learned
to poison the earth by opening blossoming
empires of color. The bees made golden
by pollen produced the honey that drove
the foraging Macedonians mad
in Alexander's campaign.
Then petals fell in legion;
soon there were just the endless acts
of blossoming holding the flowery world
together.

        Bliss exists outside
of time; it lives in eternal moments
inside and outside of war. It knows
the bloom of dust borne up by the bullet
that misses its mark, and leaps in joy
as the target stumbles beyond the sights.
It is one and is always winning.
It only demands complete surrender.

Lisken Van Pelt Dus

I'm interested in the seen and the unseen, the known and the unknown, the graspable and the elusive. How, for example, do we experience love? In the body, certainly, and in the mind... but somewhere more than this, too. Love is not contained; it exists between and among and elsewhere as well. It's the same with the full truth of all experience.

If you get a sense of that third dimension from one of my poems, then I'm happy. Poetry is a way for me to stay stubborn, to resist becoming numb to the inherent richness of experience. It forces me to pay attention and to be open. It forces me to let things in. It asks me to make space for strangeness, metaphor, even metamorphosis.

For me, doing this successfully is a matter of balance. An early name for the style of karate that I practice can be translated "half-hard, half-soft" – one must both control and allow, exert and release. This is the same equilibrium I seek with language when writing poetry.

Obviously, as the poet there are many elements that I direct, especially in revision. But I'm most satisfied with a poem when it also surprises me.

Fortunately, poems can be quite willing to do this, if they feel invited. Sometimes it is when I am attending particularly to the sounds and rhythms of my lines that they come up with some unexpected insight. Or something unforeseen might be revealed as I play with line breaks. Or here's my biggest procedural trick, as it were: I almost always work with a word bank, picking words that lift off the pages of whatever poetry book I'm reading that day and trying to work them into my draft. Often, they open up new channels for my poems that I would not have found without them.

Here, try it, with a sampling of words pulled from my poems in this folio. May they lead you to many surprises and to a rich dose of the uncontainable.

turtle – wings – even – body – sky – permeable – hands – knowing – once – river – each

It Began Without Either of Us Knowing

The knowing hid in the lace of our shadows
Swallows flew in and out of our mouths
Built nests in our throats

We followed the birds into chimneys
Flower-pots held our histories
The sky threaded with geranium scent held our histories
We weren't sure what was past and what was future
So we were often silent
We watched breath move in and out of us

Like water filling the bowl of the lake
We never knew who was following whom
Night grew late while we lost ourselves
Once I walked alone not knowing where
A sparrow kept me company

Shade and sun were two different worlds
It was enough to frighten us
We could hear wings, feel the air rush
Still the knowing was behind us

Morning would come again and again
Each time the sky was a new arrangement
For a long time we watched the birds
They were never predictable
They wove us into each other
No, we were already woven

The Latch Once Lifted

Light opens, vertical
like your body, your
shape but growing
and glowing as who would not
want to – so
you are willing
to risk desert, the scorch
of it, its lack
of hiding places.
You'll be a lizard
surviving
in a dry arroyo,
each yesterday washed away
by flooding light.

This River As One

Lick your palms: you'll taste it, your
ocean nature fooled into a narrow course

like my precious river here.
It's not difficult to imagine it as one

with all the other rivers, all molecules shared:
what's Orinoco now the Loire next week,

the Mississippi's roil flown in from China's Yangtze,
what's warm once cold, what's salty soon dried

free of sediment – not quite the sleight
of transubstantiation, but still, you get the point

if you keep going back, from flood to stream
to drop, to atom, quark, and spirit. If you go

small enough, even the hard among us:
invisible, passed through like liquid, easy.

Self-Portrait as Aquifer

As if flesh were permeable –

    not flesh exactly, but the whole body
    we carry around,
               what we feel with –

like rock rain-sodden, permeable
channeler
        (willing, unwilling)

    of water's need
    to be going somewhere

    like me right now
    wanting to go out in the rain—

how could I have known how deep

        you would enter me?

In Both Hands

Like one of the Magi bearing gifts,
for two nights in a row I have shown up
with a turtle, and no good reason for it,
no one to give it to. Even in the dreams
I have been puzzled, cradling the creature
in both hands, its mottled carapace
domed like a miniature arc of Earth
tessellated with tectonic plates. Well,
it drifted to me somehow, and so
I carry it, and have nothing to say
to those who question me about it.
Exploration is an act of will initially
but then you just have to take what you get
and tend it, from favorite coffee mug
to high wind sponging the sky grey
on grey. Even the neighbor yelling
at his dogs – or his wife – is a gift,
something that belongs to this life only.
I don't remember if my turtle
stuck his head out from his roof
but I think he must have. I think
it was me with the closed eyes: I called
Marco! and his voice answered *Polo!*
Polo! and when I found him I brushed
pollen from his shell into the breeze
and I brought the turtle with me
wherever I was going, surprised
at how little a life weighs
though it fills up both my hands.

How to Become the Moon

Scour an orchard for the perfect apple. Pick it and polish it. Sink your teeth into it, and swallow yourself into its taste, the sweet and pucker of it, like childhood. Remember how to scull into the air, feet rising off the ground, body no longer sodden weight but weightless god, your elbows and hands working like wings. The sky is not a ceiling, but open forever, a frame of infinite dimensions. Fill any piece of it, string yourself from cloud to star. Become a parabola, a crescent, a circle. Feel the halves of you, how they are equal, how you can face the flame or shun it. Forget what it is to know corners, the closing of them. You will fear no more darkness, your oceans crystallized and cooled under your crust. See how your surface remembers for you, records the marks of your history, its craters and bites.

Lisa J. Cihlar

A number of years ago I read two prose poems: "A Story about the Body" by Robert Hass, and "The Testy Pony" by Zachary Schomburg, and fell for them—hard. Since then I have only written a few lined poems; the majority of my poems have been housed in lovely, little boxes of prose. But either way, my work is filled with vivid imagery, a strong sense of place, and the desire, in many of them, to make ugly things beautiful with words.

The poems in this collection are all set in a cold place. When I was in the seventh grade, our science teacher, Mr. Kring, took us on a field trip to see some of the special geography of Door County, Wisconsin. All those years ago and I still remember the awe I felt when we scrambled up a rocky out-cropping and Mr. Kring pointed out the scratches on the surface of the rock where the last glacier had left its mark. All of the poems in this group were written in the winter that gets awfully long here in southern Wisconsin. I imagine the end of the world as we know it as the next ice age cometh. And maybe the sun is dying.

I noticed after I put these poems together that the world I created was matriarchal. Woman centered poems certainly come from my being female, but I also think that in the end it will take women to save the world. And women to tell the stories of the past. Memory keepers if you will. I have been asked where I get my ideas for individual poems. I don't have a good answer for that. Broadly it is a word, an image, or a memory that gets me going. I recently found out that an old acquaintance of mine died. I know that when this man was young, he and a friend were camping out west when a grizzly bear ripped into their tent, and dragged away his friend, who was found dead the next day. I don't know how yet, but that memory is going to show up in a poem in some way.

The next question I'm asked is: What does this poem mean? The answer for that is that sometimes I know, and sometimes I don't know. But usually I can make something up on the spot to satisfy the questioner. I don't think the poet always has to know what a poem means. I will leave that to eighth grade English teachers and their beleaguered students.

Eskars and Drumlins

These petroglyphs carved into the limestone of the Niagara Escarpment by the last glacier are signposts showing her way home. Under this shelf of rock she tucks a wind-up mouse and a wind-up ladybug. The mechanism is broken in both, but the little rubber wheels still turn on the bug that is orange and bigger than the rodent. This land hump is a knife-edge slicing between growing lavender and killing lavender. She never gives up. Sometimes she lets him help by digging holes in the chalky soil. More often she sends him to the dovecote to leave seeds and fresh water. Everything about him hurts her memory. Everything in her memory is lies and she tells them without a blush to strangers at the greenhouse where they sell dreams.

Wind-Chill Factor

We shadowbox in front of the pale nightlight. Everything is elongated at 2 a.m. He chews his claws and spits the sharp points on the carpet next to the couch when he thinks I am not watching. I am always watching for wildness. He is thick around the waist and can't find a belt to fit so we tie two together to make one. He expects to move up to a blue belt in karate class. He says it matches my eyes. We are also taking skeleton lessons to prepare for the next Winter Olympics in Russia. I have yet to tell him that bears are not allowed. He expects that everyone will assume his fur is just a heavy winter coat. In the glow of the shell shaped nightlight, this might be a mistake I can understand. Besides, the Russians love bears. But then he hugs me and I am no longer sure. If nothing else, we are not affected by the cold.

The Last Katydid

I keep the last katydid in a brass cricket-box. The bear in my life likes to listen to the chirping. It is calming. I don't know how long I can fake it. Hollyhocks have stopped self-seeding, all of the crickets have died, and the hens' combs are frostbitten. They are still laying five pure white eggs and one blue egg each day. The chicks were darling fluffs at the co-op. I can't remember their fancy names. Just that I wanted lemon curd and bright golden yolks. Eggs are both sun and moon. My bear desires profiteroles filled with custard. If katydids have mates they lay eggs that overwinter in the ground. Without a partner we will lose the green that is only katydid. I obsess. I live with a bear which makes it easy. We keep a fire burning to stave off hibernation. Neither of us has enough fat to last the long winter. Here at the edge of the forest, creatures nose around my coop and there is some unsettled cackling at midnight. Bear love is black and furry, nearsighted and toothy. And bold, always bold.

Digging Up the Mastodon

Pine trees press south, ever south. It smells of balsam fir all the time now. Old oaks and maples die, tip over, compost into duff. The last giant willow topples in an arctic blast. There are bones wrapped in rooty embrace. Secret smoke signals spread the word. A hairy elephant. Spin a tusk to see who kisses whom. Losers shiver under skins donated by lions and tigers and bears. Someone loves Tollund Man enough to walk the almost frozen bog where artesian springs make it dangerous. Minerals in the water will dissolve pocket change so risen bodies become impossible to date.

The Art of Joinery

Strangers come into my house and talk to me about other strangers. They hunch cross-legged in corners and praise a woodworker who makes perfect dovetails or uses butterflies made of cherry as decorative joiners. There is some fear in the outermost edges of my brain when they get up and begin pacing. Their long black cowboy coats are made of vulture feathers which can only be seen in reverse in the hall-closet mirror. They want nothing but listeners as far as I can tell, and they are not waiting for me to die. I shoo them out the windows into the violent evening. The next morning I sweep up wood curls and sawdust.

Tell Us a Story, They Cry

Stars snap in the cold air. Every night the northern lights make unkept promises. We learned that ice and snow is never white but blue and green. All the warm colors have leaked from the world. Explaining pink is impossible because there is no such thing. In the front of the beginning of this long winter there were snow-angels. That is what talemother told us. Everyone has given up on angels now. Same with laughter and highjinx. Fishing though the ice in August was a lark once, as was walking at midnight because it is never dark when stars reflect off snow. Everyone wants to get closer to the fire when the hoarfrost needles in around the doorframe. The stories told there are white bears and blood and teeth.

Alison Stone

I believe poetry should give the reader pleasure – pleasure of sound, of play, of unexpected language. The pleasure of recognition. At the same time, poems don't have to be pleasant. They can bite. They can hurt. The best ones often do.

I always wanted to be a rock star, but gave up before starting due to lack of talent. This is odd, since I was a punk rocker and believed anyone with enough integrity and passion could do it. But being asked to lip-synch in chorus had scarred deep. I couldn't get past that, so poems became my way to sing.

There can be a split between "street poetry" and "formal poetry," with the former often lacking craft and the latter being frightfully dull. I seek to bridge that gap, to keep the initial gut impulse while pressing language to see what it can do. I love form – ghazals, sestinas. I love pantoums for their repetition and sonnets for their voltas. Even when I'm working in free verse, I often find bits of form creeping in.

Good political poems are hard to write, though the world certainly needs more of them. Of course, telling the truth of the experience of the less powerful is, in itself, a political act. I wish I could write overtly political poems well. Since I can't, I don't (with rare exceptions.)

Experience happens in the body. Every day in my work as a Gestalt therapist I see the power of trading abstractions and ideas for felt experience. Poetry works the same way. It's visceral, primal, holistic. Like therapy, it changes us.

I try to read poetry every day. There's so much great stuff out there. The more I read, the easier it is to write.

Writing is joyful, natural. Revision, which I do obsessively, uses a very different energy. I can do fifty drafts of a poem, or more. I'll keep changing a word or a line break to get the right sound. But once a poem is published in a book, that's it.

YES

Love is a room I enter sideways.
Roots of gut, branches of bone,
our bodies burn like trees.

Our faces have left us.
Whatever ties us to our names has vanished
in the owl's beak.
Boneless, we are maggots feeding
underneath the rock of the dark.
Our mouths open to coral and stars.

Hunger

They have to wait to bury my mother
until my daughter stops nursing.
She had slept in a padded basket

while I stood wooden between my husband and my father;
people droned my mother's praises
and the coffin loomed.

Now she wakes and roots, all
hunger. A stranger takes us
to the rabbi's study. Amid clutter

of paper and books, I lift my black shirt. Broken,
numb, I cannot imagine my body
will respond, but her latch draws milk down.

She sucks dreamily. New to this world,
she knows nothing but a mother
who drips tears on her still-closing skull.

Her eyes flicker open and shut. Someone knocks,
asks me to hurry. I rub my daughter's back.
Her eyes stay closed now

but the fierce gums clamp.
I wait. The knot in my throat starts to soften.
As long as she holds on, nothing is

final. The drive to the grave
postponed, my mother is still above ground, here
with her new grandchild and me.

Cribs and Falling Coconuts

My neighbor glares at my new dog.
A puppy, she's all wiggle and licks,
but wide jaw and brindle fur mark her
a menace to our neighborhood.
Those things kill kids you know.

Pit bulls kill 2.48 people per year.
Forty children per year drown
in five gallon buckets. Also per year,
More than 100 people choke to death
on ball point pens. My neighbor
has a five gallon bucket. She probably

has ballpoint pens.
Though the pup offers her belly,
fear chews through facts, digs
under reassurances. Grabs
and shakes and won't let go.
She seems sweet,
but aren't you scared?

Terrified—
of bomb plots, in-law visits,
hospitals, heights, Lyme ticks,
pesticides, the Christian Right.

Now, learning walk-to-heel (step,
call, leash tug, kissing noises,
praise, kneel, praise)
I'm calm, focused, lost in dog.
Oblivious to future horrors.
Fear's jaws, for the moment, slacken.

Sweets

I love you like an anorexic teenager
loves chocolate. All boundaries and mastered
greed. Hips sharp, she's memorized
the recipes for Devil's Food, Black Forest --
beats butter and eggs, spoons batter
into greased tins. She won't try a bite, her empty
fork aimed at God.

Vulnerable to you, I might become
one of those moon-faced women, wounded
and obvious, spilling out of a loose dress.

Some nights when we hold each other,
my clenched teeth relax. I taste
how it would be to love you
like a glutton guzzles milkshakes, gobbles
slabs of syrup-drizzled cake. Dizzy
with sugar. All those bony
years of discipline undone.

Denial

Not often. Not much. Not that inde-
cent thing. Not you. The witness lied.
(Your convoluted alibis. Your plea deal.)
Erasures and revisions lead
to an Egyptian river town. There, facts alien
to your desires drown. Eager deni-
zen, you spoon sky into a bowl and dine
on cloudiness, sink down, lean
back, soothed by the smudged line
connecting want and is. (Your idle
swimmer's arms. Your wings of lead.)

Perimenopause

The moon
           unbinds her cords

Rogue wave, my body
    crests and crashes

to the staccato rhythm
  of last chances

womb frantic
with final eggs

Mommy, hurry up!
the children cry

Their sea glass eyes
               Their arms of sand

Beth Copeland

My poems attempt to pair concepts that may seem antithetical, such as remembering and forgetting, holding on and letting go, and living and dying. As I processed my emotions about my parents' dementia and deaths, I wanted to remember them while at the same time forgetting what was painful; to hold on to my love for them while releasing what I'd lost; and to preserve our family history while living without my parents.

"Featherweight Singer" tracks the journey of my mother's sewing machine from the United States to Japan. Just as she stitched fabric together to make dresses for her daughters, the poem is an attempt to sew together the East and the West, the past and the present, and the living and the dead.

"Kintsugi" describes the short-term memory loss my mother developed in her 80's; she could vividly remember a Japanese friend she hadn't seen in twenty-five years but forgot to check her mailbox at the assisted living facility. Like a broken vessel mended with gold, the poem preserves my fractured perceptions of my mother.

I wrote "Keeping Time" after visiting my father in a nursing home. He had Alzheimer's and frequently lost his belongings. I discovered that his watch was missing and later, remembered how I loved to listen to his watch ticking when I was a small child. The watch became a metaphor for my father's heart, which was still beating but would stop.

"Sandhills Gold" was inspired by my father's beekeeping hobby. In the poem, the honey solidifies in the jar as we become stuck in grief or becomes amber in an amulet of a pleasant moment preserved. Eventually, it flows, as the lines of the poem flow and grief is released.

All four of the poems are written as a series of couplets that end with a single line, reflecting the absence of a loved one. I didn't deliberately structure the poems that way, but it's probably not an accident that they turned out that way.

Featherweight Singer

My mother ferried her sewing machine
across the Pacific four times, stitching

continents as if
they were linen scraps—America

to Asia, Asia to America—following
Daddy as he exchanged his

version of heaven
for a suitcase of Shinto

scrolls. I fell
asleep to the white noise of that

black machine, to the song of steady
seams like wind in cottonwoods

or rain on rafters, to my mother's breathing
when I climbed her bed after bad dreams.

My sisters and I wore our Sunday best—puffed
sleeves, gathered skirts, and sashes

sewn on the Featherweight Singer as we slept.
When I was fourteen, she tried to teach me

to pin Simplicity patterns to fabric and cut
on printed lines, but I—sullen

and careless, too young
to believe I'd ever be alone—

thought she'd never leave. On her old
machine, I sew silk

infinity scarves for sisters
and friends from vintage Varanasi

saris, listening to my
mother's song in the rise

and fall of the needle and whir
of the unwinding spool. *World without*

end, amen, amen.

Kintsugi

Mother's Japanese friends
send cards she forgets

to open—prints of blond
birds flying

over turquoise waves, pine branches
burdened with snow. Her mailbox,

stuffed with letters
and junk. I slice

into an envelope and pluck a handwritten
note from Kinko-san: *I have not heard*

from you. I am worried. You are so
old. Mother snorts, *She's*

almost as old as I am!
and we laugh

at what's lost
in translation. She forgets bills,

to brush her teeth or swallow
her thyroid pills and Lipitor

but remembers Kinko-san
from long ago. Should I write to say you're

okay? *I'll do it
later*, but she won't. She stares

at a maple for hours when I'm
not here, her hair a corona

of uncombed
dandelion seeds. Should I

laugh or cry? Like a broken
bowl mended with molten

gold, she's more
beautiful than before. I hold

her in the heart
of my heart

where she's whole.

Keeping Time

In the blue wheelchair, his eyes
open when I enter. Does

he know me? Maybe
he dives into the resemblance

to a snapshot
pinned to his wall. At 94,

he drifts in and out of distant time
zones and forgotten memories. We graze

National Geographic, snowflakes, maple
leaves, and stars magnified

thousands of degrees. The clock
doesn't advise

me to stay or leave, his watch
somewhere still keeping time. When

I was small, I'd hop onto his lap
while he held it to my ear,

the gold warm from his wrist.
As I listened to its ticking, I believed

he could hold back
time forever, a pulse that

would never stop.

Sandhills Gold

... in the Sandhills of North Carolina,
a few lucky beekeepers strike blue gold.
—Chick Jacobs

The year Daddy died, beekeepers found blue
honey in their hives. How it turns

blue or why it only happens
here no one knows. Some

think bees feed on bruised huckleberries, scuppernongs
or kudzu blossoms. Too far inland, Daddy

never found it in the forty-five years
he kept hives. In the nursing home,

I talked blue honey into blue eyes that
stared back in a blur

of lost memory and sleep. What
was he thinking? I spoke

of his veiled hat and long gloves,
bellowing hives

with smoke so he could pull combs and
honey from inside, and pour sourwood

into old Mason jars in slow motion
like the lengthening summer day

when the sky was so delphinium
it could be music, or the blue

shadow that followed me through the doorway
into the buzzing of bees when I

was thirteen, crying behind the pear tree because
I wasn't popular enough to be

May Queen. This is what I choose
to keep against forgetting:

You'll always
be my queen,

he said, bending
to kiss my forehead. I carry

that moment like a bee
in amber on a gold chain

above my heart to ward off wintering
broods and dark swarms, a queen without

a country or hive, standing in slanted light
as bees droned

around my head, weaving a crown of wings
and buzzing with sweetness.

*****

Grief like honey left too long in the jar,
like the pint we bought last year

from a beekeeper who used to sell pot,
in the pantry all winter flanked by bottles

of blackstrap and Hungry Jack
crystallizing in the dark,

too solid to spoon onto bread unless you melt it
in water on the stove. Impatient,

I spread the gold grains on my toast, remembering
when he was alive and it

poured in slow
measures onto my mother's home-baked bread. One

summer he visited me in Chicago after robbing
his hive of a quart jar of sourwood

honey, his ankles so
swollen from stings he slept with his feet propped

on pillows. I want this
grief to dissolve like a lemon

lozenge on my tongue, I want
to taste the sweetness

of mornings
before sorrow, anger, and remorse

soured my vision of being
young and oblivious to his

pain, I want my words to flow
like a vein

onto the blue-lined page as holy
honey flowed from his white

hives onto our bread, tongues, lives.

Peter Ludwin

My aesthetic varies depending on the type of poem I am writing, whether narrative, lyric or a combination of the two. Nevertheless, it is informed by certain convictions. Central among them is the function of monosyllabic words in English language poetry. One need only refer to poets as separated in time as Shakespeare and Dylan Thomas to perceive this. Because English at its base is a Germanic language in which consonants play a leading emphasis, monosyllabics combined with a sprinkling of two-syllable words give poetry in English rhythmic power and punch. As Scottish poet Alastair Reid stated in a workshop years ago, "Listen to how it sounds on the ear!"

So it begins with the character of the English language and specific word choices used to make a poem come alive and get off the ground. Each poem is its own unique universe. When I began writing, I wanted to sound contemporary, but with a sense of music. Rhythm is important to me, and I've been influenced in that direction not only by poets I admire, but also by my being a musician and having grown up near the sounds of trains and tides. Some of those poets include Rilke, Theodore Roethke, Dylan Thomas, James Dickey, James Wright, Federico García Lorca, Pablo Neruda, Mark Doty, Pattiann Rogers, Joseph Stroud, Robert Wrigley and Joseph Fasano.

Lorca and Neruda are fabulous mentors in the use of imaginative metaphors that resonate below the level of surface awareness. They tend to make *emotional* sense rather than sequential rational sense. There is more than one way to "understand" a poem. And I am always partial to *flow*, much as a mountain stream rushes and then slows before picking up velocity again. I like to use the physical world as a jumping off point for interior exploration, whether aesthetic, ethical or spiritual. When a person tells me, "You put me right *there* in your poem!" I know I've done my job, and that the poem has passed the "So what?" test.

Arrow Flight

Those old Germanic tribes knew how to do it right.
When Beowulf died they carried his body down
to the beach, placed it on a boat with his armor,
torched it and set it adrift.
Then they straggled back up the sand,
got roaring drunk around the bonfires and stayed
the night telling stories of their comrade.
By morning all was ashes: Beowulf, the boat,
the smoldering fires, silent tongues of his warriors
    buried in sleep.

When they burned you, Father, they removed you shrouded
from the hospital, stole along crumbling, graffiti-scarred walls
    like lepers
whose ravaged shadows fell misshapen on the cobblestones.
You couldn't see their eyes drain the blood
from dark rivers, couldn't hear the jackal's bark
when they tossed the ashes like an old, broken-spring
clock that lacked even the memory of leaves.
Bearing you on no shield except the tarnished plate
of indifference they filled out their forms.

No one raised a glass.
No one knew a story to tell.

None saw, in the bandit's storm of dust,
a gazelle outrun mirage.

Inside the Blue Mosque, Istanbul

Say the word aloud, say *blue*,
and the mind teems with guests:
Renoir, Vermeer, Gainsborough's *Blue Boy*,
Picasso's Blue Period, the lines
from a Mark Doty crab poem:
a shocking Giotto blue.

Say *blue*, and a marlin taildances on the water,
a slide guitar spells heartache in plural.
Woke up this mornin', I believe I'll dust my broom.
Frida lives on in *la Casa Azul.*
And the beggar trapped in a hash dream
haze hails bands of blue men from the Sahara.

Say *blue*, and doors swing wide open.
To speak it here adds yet another
tile to the thousands already present.
Did Gershwin divine such a rhapsody?
Such a dazzling faience mosaic?
Or is blue encoded in our cells,

a script for the primal color of being?
Look around. When you left your shoes
at the door, didn't you slough off
your skin so blue could breathe,
could curl phantom-like among the pillars,

a counterpoint
to the slow, steady rhythm
of a cobbler tapping out his blood
beat in the bazaar, circa 1650?
Blue. It haunts the back alleys,

a companion for the road, for the long haul,
for daughter and courtesan a final recumbent address.
First water, last silence, the country in between.
Blue Danube. Blue bayou. *Cordon bleu.*
The heron and the kingfisher. Blue.

Walking to Watmough Bay

Down through a long corridor of trees
    we pass
wearing a mantle of low clouds.
    Scattered by death,
yellow leaves decorate our hair.
    Today we transcend
our bodies. Today we inhabit
    the wind
and lie naked with rock cliffs
    plunging to the bay.
Past their season, rosehip bushes
    do not acknowledge us.
But the darkening afternoon, the slate gray
    waters of the cove—
these speak in muffled voices.
    Tiny swells
undulate the blood.
    A flute
follows gulls into winter.
    Music for two fish
we play imperceptibly, feathers brushing stone.
    Within ourselves
we are shaping what the earth
    spinning on its axis
shapes, we mold our own slow time.
    All points now
to a great shutting down of things,
    a flutter
of wings above a thin white candle
    burning
where the world unveils a minor key.

    Isn't this
what we decided lifetimes ago,
      the touch
of your rain-flecked hand
     a witness?

CARETAKERS

These old barns
lean into the storm like buffalo.

Wind between their ribs
taunts the root cellar,

snow scatters
voices in the rafters.

Wooden skeletons
speak of who is not,

who once pitched hay
on the dream floor

when tears stained the fence.
Someone here milked desire

while the cow wandered off,
someone told stories to the snake.

Mildewed, they cling to planks
rotted away by whispers.

*There is a time
and a time
and a time…*

Touch the broken boards
and those stories blaze up like rosehips

igniting the Chesaw Road,
singe your fingers like frost.

Terezin Concentration Camp, Bohemia

Near the railway spur
bones still cry for water.

And the ashes?
Who can say what roots they nourish,
what borders they have crossed?

Here the ship never sails,
the shawl cannot cover.

Tell me silence isn't the loudest voice.

When the open mouth forgets itself,
the straw man drinks his shadow.

And the moon?
Gracing a wanted poster,

an impossible price on its head.

Coal-faced, it shuns the cattle cars
rolling east on tracks of tallow.

Absence. Isn't that the surest
footprint of a crime?
The song the mockingbird teaches its young?

This rain grazes the skin like rust.

In the Crosshairs,
Comanche National Grassland

Fire sears the air this morning:
in my friend Katie's poems,
the autumn colors,
twinges in my throat and jaw.
When cancer struck at twenty-five
it bore no pain, gave no warning.
Do I now, so many years later,
harbor malignant seeds
instead of geese on the wing?

Surely the truth lies elsewhere.
In the cottonwoods, for example,
that line the Purgatoire River,
the blazing of their gold
against the white peaks
a climax fever my bones inherit
as kindling flares to match.
Or in the blueberry muffins
Katie baked with flax flour,

how butter and steaming,
crumb-filled texture melting
on the tongue felt almost too sensual,
like an itch when the blood's inflamed.
Then again, what of this ember
glowing deep within the marrow,
this coal that scores
even the most resistant wood
with blackened grooves?

There is the need to get things down,
to leave a mark, an imprint,
some sign that validates a life.

This is what the cottonwoods demand,
these stunted prairie grasses:
a voice that insists,
that announces to no one in particular,
ah, Consuelo, *mi vida*,
I was here, I sang your song.

Publication Credits

Sandra Marchetti

    "Shadow" first appeared in *Appalachian Heritage*

    "Ebb Tide" first appeared in *South Dakota Review*

    "Amberwing" first appeared in Still first appeared in *The Journal*

    "Kaleidoscope" first appeared in *Split Lip Magazine*

    "Soon" first appeared in *Mead: A Journal of Literature and Libations*

Lia Brooks

    "The Sink Eels" first appeared in *Penumbra*

    "The Flood" first appeared in *Agenda Broadsheets*

    "Elk" was a prize-winner in the Troubadour Poetry Prize and also appeared on the Coffee-House Poetry site

Lynne Thompson

    "Before We Are Full of Rue", "How I Learned Where We Come From", and "To Blackness" all appeared in *Beg No Pardon* (Perugia Press, 2007)

    "Last Elegy for the Red Dress" and "Wishbone" both appeared in *Start With a Small Guitar* (What Books Press, 2013)

    "Genesis" appeared in *Fifth Wednesday Journal*, Fall, 2013

Sharon Venezio

    "Returning #2" first appeared in *Grey Sparrow*, July 2016

    "Snapshot in Sepia", "Three Exits", and "The Flame" first appeared in *The Silence of Doorways*, Moon Tide Press, 2013

    "Disquietude" first appeared in *Spillway*, June 2013

Allan Johnston

"War Is Opened" was first published in *Modern Review*

"Meditation on Bliss" first appeared in *Poetry East*, and later appeared in *A Writers' Congress: Chicago Poets on Barack Obama's Inauguration*

"Attacking Solipsism with Flour Tortillas" appeared in *Poetry Repairs*

"The Eater of Avocadoes" appeared in *Rio*

"Ashes" has been published by *Softblow*

All five poems are from a manuscript now entitled *In a Window* that is currently circulating

Lisken Van Pelt Dus

"In Both Hands" was first published in *The Warwick Review* and republished in *What We're Made Of* (Cherry Grove Collections 2016). It also appeared as a "Poem of the Moment" on Mass Poetry's website

"Self-Portrait as Aquifer" and "The Latch First Lifted" both first appeared in the online journal *qarrtsiluni*. Both also appear in *What We're Made Of* (Cherry Grove Collections 2016)

"This River as One" appears in *What We're Made Of* (Cherry Grove Collections 2016)

Lisa Cihlar

"The Art of Joinery" originally appeared in *Yew*

"Wind-chill Factor" originally appeared in *Burnside Review*

"Digging Up the Mastodon" originally appeared in *Grey Sparrow Press*

Alison Stone

"Yes" appeared in *They Sing at Midnight* (Many Mountains Moving Press, 2003)

"Hunger" appeared in *Dangerous Enough* (Presa Press, 2014)

"Sweets" appeared in *Ordinary Magic* (NYQ Books, 2016)

Beth Copeland

"Featherweight Singer" first appeared in *America is Not the World*, a Pankhearst Press anthology, 2016

"Kintsugi" was published in *The Wide Shore: A Journal of Global Women's Poetry*, Issue Three, 2016

An earlier version of "Keeping Time" first appeared in *Kakalak 2013* and was also published in *Weatherings*, A Good Works Project, FutureCycle Press, 2015

An earlier version of the first section of "Sandhills Gold" was published as "Blue Honey" in *Naugatuck River Review*, Issue 9, Winter 2013; *New Millennium Writings*, Number Twenty-two, 2013; *Bay Leaves*, Number Thirty-nine, 2013; *The Southern Poetry Anthology, Volume VII: North Carolina*, 2014; and *Shining Rock Poetry Anthology*, Spring 2015. An earlier version of the second section of "Sandhills Gold" was published in *Tar River Poetry*, Volume 54, Number 2, Spring 2015

Peter Ludwin

"In the Crosshairs, Comanche National Grassland" originally appeared in *Cottonwood*, and later appeared in *A Guest in All Your Houses*

"Walking to Watmough Bay" originally appeared in *The Paradigm Poets Anthology*

"Inside the Blue Mosque, Istanbul" originally appeared in *Nimrod*, and later appeared in *Rumors of Fallible Gods*

"Terezin Concentration Camp, Bohemia" originally appeared in *The Raven Chronicles*, and later appeared in *Rumors of Fallible Gods*

"Caretakers" was published by *Common Ground Review*

"Arrow Flight" was published by *San Pedro River Review*

Contributor Notes

Sandra Marchetti is the author of *Confluence*, a full-length collection of poetry from Sundress Publications (2015). She is also the author of four chapbooks of poetry and lyric essays, including *Sight Lines* (Speaking of Marvels Press, 2016), *Heart Radicals* (ELJ Publications, 2016), *A Detail in the Landscape* (Eating Dog Press, 2014), and *The Canopy* (MWC Press, 2012). Sandra's poetry appears widely in *Subtropics, Ecotone, Green Mountains Review, Word Riot, Blackbird, Southwest Review*, and elsewhere. Her essays can be found at *The Rumpus, Words Without Borders, Mid-American Review, Whiskey Island*, and other venues. Currently, she is a Lecturer in Interdisciplinary Studies at Aurora University outside of her hometown of Chicago.

Lia Brooks's poetry has been published in the UK and the US. Some of these publications include; *Poetry London, Lily Lit Review, Antiphon, Mslexia, Agenda, Penumbra, Qarrtsiluni* and *Magma Newsletters*. Her poetry has been twice nominated for a Pushcart Prize, short-listed for the Bridport Prize, prize-winner in the Troubadour Poetry Prize and highly commended in the *Mslexia* Pamphlet Competition. Lia Brooks was born in Epsom, Surrey, and currently lives in Southampton, UK, with her partner and two sons.

In 2015, **Lynne Thompson** was awarded an Individual Artist Fellowship from the City of Los Angeles and she is the author of two full-length poetry collections, *Beg No Pardon*, winner of the Perugia Press Prize and the Great Lakes Colleges Association's New Writers Award, and *Start With A Small Guitar* (What Books Press). Thompson's poems have appeared in the recent anthology, *Coiled Serpent, Poets Arising from the Cultural Quakes & Shifts of Los Angeles* as well as the literary journals *Ecotone, North American Review*, and *Solstice Literary Magazine* which selected one of her poems, "Politics", as winner of its Stephen Dunn Poetry Prize. Thompson is Reviews and Essays Editor of the literary journal, *Spillway*.

Sharon Venezio, born and raised in New Jersey, moved to California in 1995 where she studied both psychology and creative writing. For six years she was a member of the Writers At Work poetry workshop. During this time she also co-directed the Valley Contemporary Poets, arranging and hosting poetry readings in the San Fernando Valley. She is the author of *The Silence of Doorways* (March 2013, Moon Tide Press), a full-length poetry collection. Her poems have appeared in numerous journals, including *Spillway, Bellevue Literary Review, Reed,* and elsewhere. She is also featured in the anthology *Wide Awake: Poets of Los Angeles and Beyond* as well as the anthology *Stone, River, Sky: an Anthology of Georgia Poems.* She lives in Los Angeles where she works as a behavior analyst specializing in autism. Read more at sharonvenezio.com

Originally from southern California, **Allan Johnston** earned his M.A. in Creative Writing and his Ph.D. in English from the University of California, Davis. His poems have appeared in over sixty journals, including *Poetry, Poetry East, Rattle,* and *Rhino.* He has published one full-length poetry collection (*Tasks of Survival,* 1996) and three chapbooks (*Northport,* 2010; *Departures,* 2013; *Contingencies,* 2015). His awards include an Illinois Arts Council Fellowship, finalist placement in competitions sponsored by New Writers, the Roberts Writing Awards Foundation, and other agencies, a Pushcart Prize nomination (2009) and First Prize in Poetry in the Outrider Press Literary Anthology competition (2010). He now teaches writing and literature at Columbia College and DePaul University in Chicago. He also reads or has read for *Word River, r.kv.r.y,* and the Illinois Emerging Poets competition, and is co-editor of *JPSE: Journal for the Philosophical Study of Education.* Articles published in *Twentieth Century Literature, College Literature,* and several other journals have explored the poetry and writings the Beats, Robinson Jeffers, James Joyce, Robert Lowell, Kenneth Rexroth, and Gary Snyder, among other writers.

Lisken Van Pelt Dus was raised in England, the US, and Mexico, and now lives in western Massachusetts, where she teaches high school and martial arts. Her poetry can be found in such journals as *Conduit, The South Carolina Review,* and *upstreet,* and has earned awards from *Cider Press Review, Atlanta Review,* and others. Her chapbook, *Everywhere at Once,* was published by Pudding House Press in 2009, and a full-length book, *What We're Made Of,* was released by Cherry Grove Collections in May 2016.

Lisa J. Cihlar's poems have appeared in *Blackbird, Gargoyle Magazine, South Dakota Review, Crab Creek Review,* and *Mid-American Review.* Her three chapbooks are *The Insomniac's House* from Dancing Girl Press, *This is How She Fails* from Crisis Chronicles Press, and *When I Pick Up My Wings from the Dry Cleaner* from Blue Light Press.

Alison Stone is the author of five poetry collections, including *Ordinary Magic* (NYQ Books, 2016), *Dangerous Enough* (Presa Press 2014), and *They Sing at Midnight,* which won the 2003 Many Mountains Moving Poetry Award and was published by Many Mountains Moving Press. Her poems have appeared in *The Paris Review, Poetry, Ploughshares, Barrow Street, Poet Lore,* and a variety of other journals and anthologies. She has been awarded *Poetry's* Frederick Bock Prize and *New York Quarterly's* Madeline Sadin award. She is also a painter and the creator of The Stone Tarot. A licensed psychotherapist, she has private practices in NYC and Nyack. She is currently editing an anthology of poems on the Persephone/Demeter myth.

Beth Copeland lived in Japan, India, and North Carolina as a child. Her first full-length poetry book, *Traveling Through Glass*, received the 1999 Bright Hill Press Poetry Book Award. *Transcendental Telemarketer*, her second poetry collection, was published by BlazeVOX books in 2012 and received the runner up award in the North Carolina Poetry Council's 2013 Oscar Arnold Young Award for best poetry book by a North Carolina writer. Her poems have been widely published in literary journals and have received awards from *Atlanta Review*, *New Millennium Writings*, *North American Review*, and *Peregrine*. Her poems have been featured on *PBS NewsHour* and have been nominated for a Pushcart Prize. She is employed as assistant professor of English at Methodist University. She lives in a log cabin in rural North Carolina.

Peter Ludwin is the recipient of a Literary Fellowship from Artist Trust and the W.D. Snodgrass Award for Endeavor and Excellence in Poetry. His first book, *A Guest in All Your Houses*, was published in 2009 by Word Walker Press. His second collection is *Rumors of Fallible Gods*, a two-time finalist for the Gival Press Poetry Award that was published in 2013 by Presa Press. His new book, *Gone to Gold Mountain*, was published in August, 2016 by MoonPath Press.

A participant for twelve years in the San Miguel Poetry Week in Mexico, where he studied under such noted poets as Mark Doty, Tony Hoagland, Joseph Stroud and Robert Wrigley, Ludwin was the Second Prize Winner of the 2007-2008 Anna Davidson Rosenberg Awards and a finalist during the same period for *The Comstock Review's* Muriel Craft Bailey Memorial Award. In 2010 he was nominated for a Pushcart Prize. In 2011 he received Special Merit Recognition from *The Comstock Review*, and that same year *Soundings Review* named him its Reader's Choice winner in the spring/summer issue. In 2016 he was a finalist in poetry for the Tucson Festival of Books Literary Awards, the Second Place poetry prize winner of the Kay Snow Writing Awards sponsored by Willamette Writers, and the First Prize winner of the Muriel Craft Bailey Memorial Award, judged by Marge Piercy. His work has appeared in many journals, including *Atlanta Review, The Bitter Oleander, The Comstock Review, Crab Orchard Review, Nimrod, North American Review* and *Prairie Schooner,* to name a few. A world traveler who has journeyed by canoe to visit remote Indian families in the Amazon Basin of Ecuador, hiked in the Peruvian Andes, thumbed for rides in Greece, bargained for goods in the markets of Marrakech and Istanbul and survived debilitating illness in China and Tibet, he is also accomplished on acoustic guitar and autoharp. He lives in Kent, Washington, where he works for the Parks Department.

Glass Lyre Press

exceptional works to replenish the spirit

Glass Lyre Press is an independent literary publisher interested in technically accomplished, stylistically distinct, and original work. Glass Lyre seeks diverse writers that possess a dynamic aesthetic and an ability to emotionally and intellectually engage a wide audience of readers.

Glass Lyre's vision is to connect the world through language and art. We hope to expand the scope of poetry and short fiction for the general reader through exceptionally well-written books, which evoke emotion, provide insight, and resonate with the human spirit.

Poetry Collections
Poetry Chapbooks
Select Short & Flash Fiction
Anthologies

www.GlassLyrePress.com

www.ingramcontent.com/pod-product-compliance
Lightning Source LLC
Chambersburg PA
CBHW021154080526
44588CB00008B/337